Clinical and Investigative Features of Cardiac Pathology

Ischaemic Heart Disease

George C Sutton
Hillingdon Hospital, Middlesex, UK

Kim M Fox
National Heart Hospital, London, UK

Current Medical Literature Ltd, London

"Clinical and Investigative Features of Cardiac Pathology".

This series is made available to you by ICI Pharmaceuticals UK as part of their commitment to continuing medical education in Cardiology.

Abbreviations

AMVL	Anterior Mitral Valve Leaflet	IVS	Interventricular Septum	N	Negative Contrast Effect
Ao	Aorta	LA	Left Atrium	PVW	Posterior Ventricular Wall
AoV	Aortic Valve	LAO	Left Anterior Oblique	RA	Right Atrium
AP	Antero-posterior	LAT	Lateral	RV	Right Ventricle
Eff	Effusion	LV	Left Ventricle	TV	Tricuspid Valve
		MV	Mitral Valve	VSD	Ventricular Septal Defect
		MVL	Mitral Valve Leaflet		

Note

The small images which accompany the text at the beginning of each chapter appear later in the chapter in a larger format.

Pathology

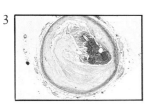

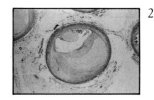

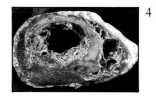

Patients with ischaemic heart disease almost always have atheroma of the coronary arteries [1] though episodes of myocardial ischaemia can occasionally result from spasm of normal coronary arteries. Rarer pathological lesions include coronary artery emboli or non-atheromatous disease of the coronary arteries or of the coronary ostia.

Although atheroma may occur to a variable extent in the coronary arterial tree, the histological pattern is consistent. Severe areas of stenosis show eccentric intimal thickening or plaques [2] containing large amounts of lipid. Lipid is often present as large pools of free cholesterol crystals separated from the lumen only by a thin layer of fibrous tissue. Thrombotic material is frequently present. Many areas of severe stenosis (>75%) have two or more lumina suggesting that they are recanalized total occlusions. Thrombotic total occlusions are due to a mass of fibrin and platelets plugging the lumen [3]. Calcification deep in the intima is common in atherosclerosis.

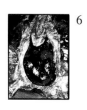

Although the initiating event causing myocardial infarction is unknown, plaque rupture leading to thrombosis of a coronary vessel may be important. This may lead to an area of muscle necrosis. The site of the infarct depends on the vessel involved. Thrombosis of the anterior descending coronary artery typically leads to an antero-septal infarct [4]. Disease in the right coronary artery results in a diaphragmatic infarct [5].

In transmural infarction, recent total occlusion due to thrombus in the supplying artery is invariably present [3]. Somewhat different pathological changes may be found when the infarct is non-transmural. These consist of sub-endocardial and focal areas of necrosis scattered throughout the ventricle. Occlusive thrombi are less consistently found.

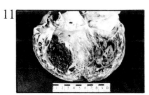

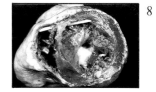

Complications of acute myocardial infarction include rupture of the left ventricle into the pericardium [6,7], ruptured interventricular septum [8], ruptured papillary muscle [9], ischaemic papillary muscle resulting in severe mitral regurgitation [10], and formation of mural thrombus within the ventricles [11,12]. Later complications include the formation of a localized left ventricular aneurysm and dilatation of the left ventricle including areas of scarring [12].

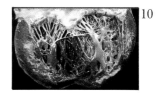

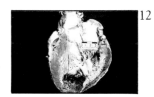

Presentation

Symptoms

Patients with ischaemic heart disease may be asymptomatic in spite of widespread severe coronary atheroma. In contrast, other patients may die suddenly without extensive disease. The usual clinical presentation includes angina, acute myocardial infarction and heart failure. Some patients may present with arrhythmias (including sudden death) without any previous symptoms due to ischaemic heart disease.

Chest pain due to myocardial ischaemia typically occurs on physical exercise or during stress probably due to myocardial oxygen demand exceeding the coronary blood supply. Episodes of chest pain may also occur at rest. Such episodes may be due to a sudden reduction in oxygen delivery to the myocardium (eg. coronary artery spasm).

Patients whose symptoms appear to be stable may develop more readily provoked pain and episodes of pain that are entirely unprovoked. Occasionally such symptoms in some patients precede the development of acute myocardial infarction, while in others the unprovoked episodes fade and the patient often returns to, or establishes, a stable pattern of chest pain.

Many patients develop myocardial infarction without premonitory symptoms. Prolonged severe chest pain is a characteristic feature. The acute development of breathlessness following infarction may be due to extensive myocardial necrosis with resulting pulmonary oedema or rarely rupture of the ventricular septum or a papillary muscle. Arrhythmias are very common in acute infarction and may be asymptomatic or result in acute breathlessness or further chest pain or syncope.

Patients with chronic ischaemic heart disease may develop heart failure without recent myocardial infarction. Such patients may have either a localized left ventricular aneurysm or left ventricular dilatation with widespread areas of scarring resulting in severely compromised left ventricular function.

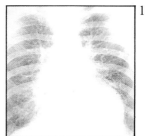

Signs

Many patients with chronic ischaemic heart disease do not have any abnormal physical signs. If there is left ventricular dysfunction, a double apical impulse will frequently be palpated and a fourth heart sound may be heard. In some patients with severe left ventricular disease, a loud pulmonary valve closure sound will be heard suggesting pulmonary hypertension. There may be a pansystolic murmur either due to chronic papillary muscle dysfunction with resultant mitral regurgitation or due to tricuspid regurgitation in patients with severe chronic heart failure with fluid retention. A third heart sound may be heard either in the patient with chronic severe ventricular dysfunction or in the acute phase of myocardial infarction with severe heart failure. The development of a pansystolic murmur shortly after acute myocardial infarction would suggest ischaemic damage to a papillary muscle, rupture of the ventricular septum or rupture of the papillary muscle. In patients with severe heart failure sinus tachycardia is common with summation of third and fourth heart sounds giving rise to the gallop rhythm. Reduced cardiac output, either as an acute or chronic complication, results in reduced perfusion of vital organs with consequent oliguria and renal failure, confusion due to poor cerebral perfusion and peripheral vasoconstriction.

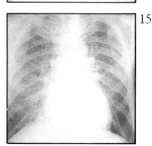

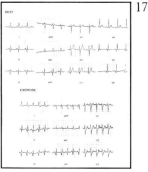

Investigations

Radiology

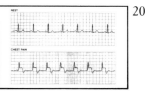

Most patients presenting with angina in the absence of left ventricular dysfunction have a normal plain chest radiograph. With long standing generalized left ventricular dysfunction or a localised left ventricular aneurysm there may be cardiomegaly and features of pulmonary venous hypertension. In about 50% of

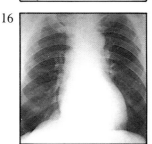

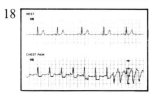

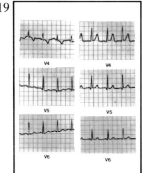

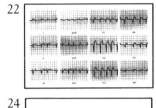

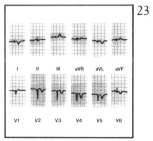

patients with a localized left ventricular aneurysm, the aneurysm may be visible on the radiograph as an abnormal bulge on the left heart border [13]. Pulmonary oedema may develop in the patient with chronic ischaemic heart disease or may follow acute myocardial infarction or one of its complications [14], such as ruptured interventricular septum or mitral regurgitation. In ruptured ventricular septum the pattern of pulmonary vessels sometimes suggests a left to right shunt [15,16].

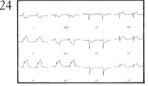

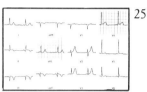

Electrocardiography

The resting ECG may often be normal. However, it may show evidence of an old myocardial infarction, ST-T abnormalities, or left bundle branch block.

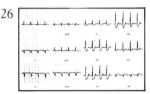

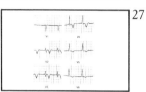

The electrocardiogram recorded during exercise is likely to show ST-segment abnormalities. The most specific change is down sloping ST-segment depression particularly in association with the development of chest pain [17]. Usually 1mm ST-segment depression is suggestive of myocardial ischaemia. The ST-segment may be upsloping, horizontal or down-sloping. Occasionally arrhythmias are recorded in association with ST-segment changes during exercise [18]. The presence of an abnormal resting ECG, particularly left bundle branch block, makes interpretation of ST-segment changes difficult.

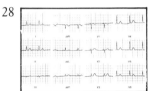

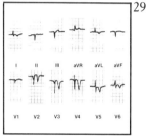

During episodes of chest pain due to myocardial ischaemia, the 12 lead ECG is likely to show ST-T wave changes that resolve when the pain is relieved [19]. The rare patient with angina due to coronary artery spasm with or without coronary atheroma (Prinzmetal's angina) shows striking ST-segment elevation during an episode of chest pain [20].

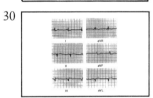

Ambulatory monitoring of ST-segments in patients with ischaemic heart disease will often show ST-T wave changes during episodes of chest pain; frequently, however, such ECG changes may be recorded in the absence of chest pain [21] and are also likely to be due to myocardial ischaemia.

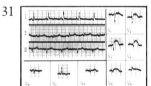

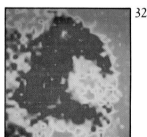

Patients who have acute myocardial infarction usually show pathological Q waves and ST-T abnormalities which evolve with time. The location of the infarct can be roughly determined from the electrocardiogram; thus an acute anterior infarct shows Q waves and ST-elevation in the anterior precordial leads (V1 to V4) with similar changes in leads 1, AVL and V5 to V6 [22]. As time passes the ST-T changes evolve into T wave inversion [23]. More localized ECG changes are seen in septal (V2–V4) or lateral (I, AVL, V5, V6) infarction. An inferior infarct shows similar changes in the inferior leads (2,3 and AVF) [24,25]. A true posterior infarction shows dominant R waves in V1 reflecting the absence of posterior forces [26].

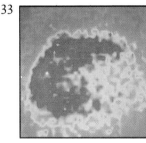

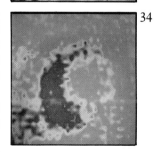

When the infarct is non-transmural (subendocardial) Q waves are not seen but there are usully striking ST-T changes which may resolve with time [27,28].

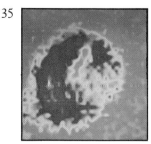

Patients with rupture of the ventricular septum following myocardial infarction usually show electrocardiographic features of a septal infarct [29] whereas those with papillary muscle infarction or ischaemia resulting in mitral regurgitation often show evidence of inferior infarction [30]. These electrocardiographic features may help in distinguishing these two complications of

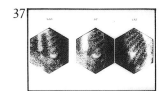

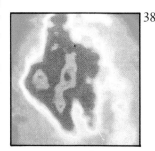

myocardial infarction clinically. Patients with a localized left ventricular aneurysm may continue to show ST-segment elevation as well as Q waves in the electrocardiogram persisting after the acute phase of myocardial infarction [31]. However, this feature is not invariable and patients with a left ventricular aneurysm may show any kind of electrocardiographic abnormality associated with coronary artery disease.

Patients with heart failure due to ischaemic heart disease almost always have ECG evidence of previous myocardial infarction, ST-T wave abnormalities or left bundle branch block at rest.

Nuclear Techniques

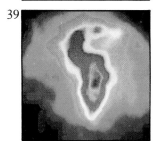

Using thallium-201 it is possible to image the myocardium during exercise or at rest. In patients with ischaemic heart disease it is often possible to show areas of the myocardium in which there is failure of uptake of this isotope due to myocardial ischaemia developing during exercise [32,33,34].

In such patients, as exercise-induced myocardial ischaemia recedes with rest, reperfusion of the isotope usually occurs after about 4 hours and the malperfused areas of myocardium visible on exercise appear normally perfused [35]. Localized thallium-201 uptake defects at rest which do not change with exercise almost invariably indicate infarcted myocardium, but the distinction between acute or chronic infarction is not possible using this technique.

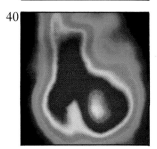

Certain radiopharmaceuticals (eg. technetium-99m labelled pyrophosphate) are preferentially taken up by irreversibly damaged or necrosed myocardial cells ('hot spot' scanning). A myocardial infarct can be visualized usually about 12–36 hours after its onset in this way [36,37].

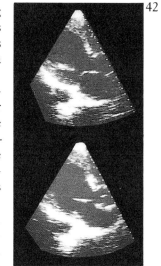

If radioactive isotopes (eg. technetium-99m labelled red cells or technetium-99m labelled human serum albumen) are injected intravenously they will become evenly distributed in the blood pool. The cardiac chambers and particularly the left ventricle can be outlined in this way. If such an investigation is carried out in a dynamic way ('gated blood pool' or 'first-pass' study), the movement of the ventricular wall can be demonstrated throughout systole and diastole [38,39]. Thus either a generalized systolic malfunction of the ventricle (as in dilated cardiomyopathy) or regional abnormalities (as in ischaemic heart disease) including a localized left ventricular aneurysm may be identified [40]. Transient regional abnormalities can be identified during exercise and imply exercise-induced regional myocardial ischaemia from significant coronary artery narrowing.

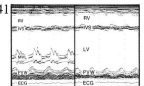

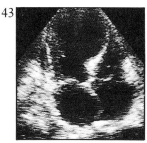

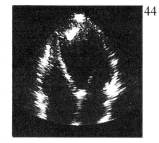

Echocardiography

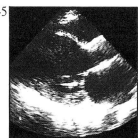

In patients with ischaemic heart disease and normal resting left ventricular function the echocardiogram is usually normal except in the rare circumstances where a recording is made during chest pain when regional wall motion abnormalities may be detected by 2-dimensional echocardiography. In those patients with chronic ischaemic heart disease who have abnormal left ventricular function, this may be detected by various techniques using echocar-

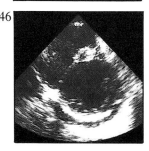

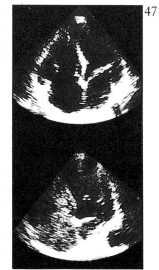

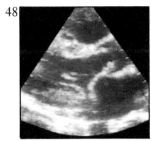

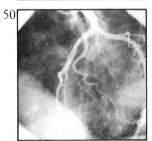

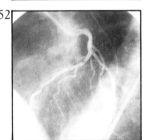

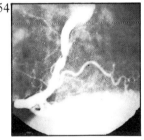

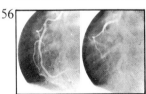

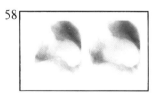

diography. M-mode echocardiography may show an increase in left ventricular dimension and reduction of wall motion when left ventricular disease is severe and generalized [41]. Sometimes, an M-mode echocardiogram showing lack of motion of either the septum or posterior wall will indicate permanent damage or scarring in those regions. 2-Dimensional echocardiography may visualize regional abnormalities within the overall function of the ventricle. Cases of extreme systolic wall thinning and/or dyskinesia are readily apparent from inspection of the systolic and diastolic images [42]. A localized left ventricular aneurysm may be detected by 2-dimensional echocardiography [43]. Thrombus within an abnormal ventricle may sometimes be seen [44].

In acute myocardial infarction, M-mode echocardiography may show outward movement of the endocardium during systole of either septum or posterior wall due in part to a reduction in wall thickness of either of these affected regions. 2-Dimensional echocardiography is usually superior in locating and determining the extent of infarcted myocardium [45].

Complications of acute myocardial infarction such as the development of a pericardial effusion [46], rupture of the ventricular septum resulting in a ventricular septal defect [47] and rupture of a papillary muscle causing flail-like motion of mitral valve leaflets may be identified using 2-dimensional echocardiography [48].

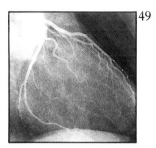

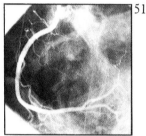

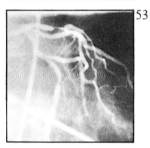

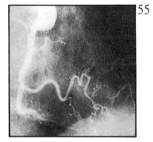

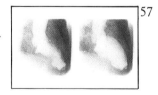

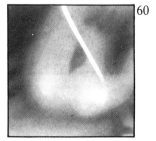

Cardiac Catheterization and Angiography

Although left ventricular pressures are often normal the most likely haemodynamic abnormality in patients with chronic ischaemic heart disease is an elevation of left ventricular end-diastolic pressure. This occurs most frequently if there is extensive chronic damage of the left ventricle or during an episode of myocardial ischaemia. In acute myocardial infarction, left ventricular end-diastolic and pulmonary capillary wedge pressure may be elevated and cardiac output reduced.

If the myocardial infarct is complicated by ventricular septal rupture, a left-to-right shunt at ventricular level will be demonstrated often with significant pulmonary hypertension. If the infarct is complicated by significant mitral regurgitation, the left atrial or pulmonary capillary wedge pressure will show a high 'V' or systolic wave. Cardiac output is likely to be reduced with either of these complications. In order to demonstrate the exact pattern of coronary artery narrowing coronary arteriography is required [49–55]. This technique may be required either in the patient with chronic ischaemic heart disease or in the acute phase of myocardial infarction. The absence of angiographically demonstrable coronary artery narrowing does not exclude the possibility of the patient having transient myocardial ischaemia. Occasionally patients with normal or near normal coronary arteries may develop coronary spasm [56].

Left ventricular angiograms may demonstrate local [57] or generalized abnormalities of left ventricular contraction, localized left ventricular aneurysm [58], mitral regurgitation, [59] and ruptured septum [60].

1 Longitudinal slice of coronary artery showing at least 80% narrowing of the lumen.

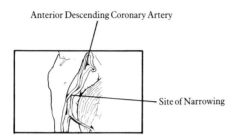

Anterior Descending Coronary Artery

Site of Narrowing

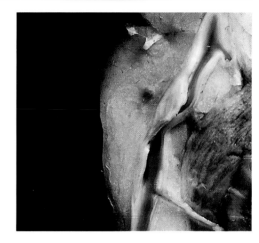

2 Narrowed coronary artery due to atherosclerosis - transverse section. The lumen is reduced to a small rather crescentic opening by a mass of intimal fibrous tissue containing lipid.

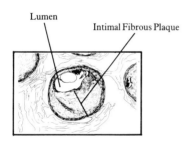

Lumen

Intimal Fibrous Plaque

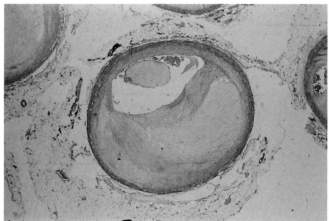

3 Thrombosed coronary artery in transverse section. The lumen is completely occluded by a mass of red thrombus. Above and to the left of the thrombus is a plaque of atheroma which contains lipid.

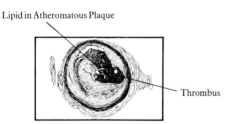

Lipid in Atheromatous Plaque

Thrombus

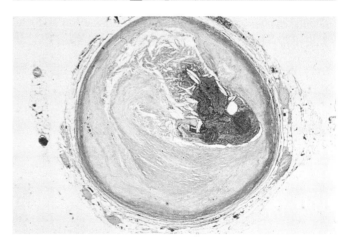

4 Transverse slice (fresh) of the ventricles. A recent (four day old) full-thickness myocardial infarction is present in the anterior wall of the left ventricle which extends into the interventricular septum.

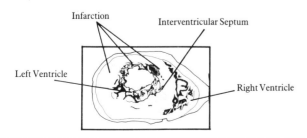

Infarction

Interventricular Septum

Left Ventricle

Right Ventricle

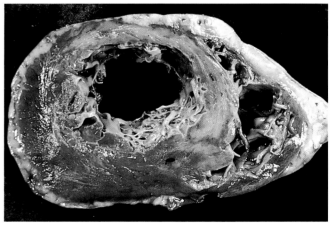

5 Slice of the ventricles stained to show succinic de-hydrogenase enzyme activity (dark). An acute infarct (diaphragmatic surface) is demonstrated as a white area due to loss of enzyme activity.

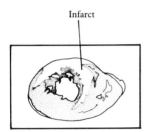

6 Pericardial sac filled with blood clot as a result of cardiac rupture due to myocardial infarction.

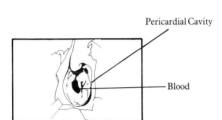

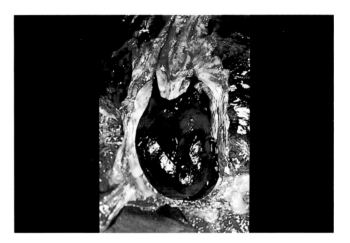

7 Rupture of the anterior wall of the left ventricle due to acute infarction.

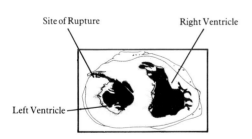

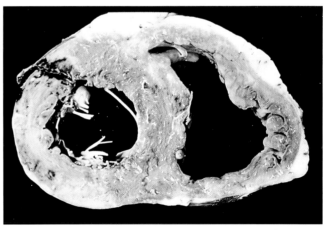

8 Acute myocardial infarction of the septum with rupture resulting in a ventricular septal defect (probe is shown passing through the defect).

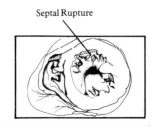

9   Acute myocardial infarction resulting in rupture of a papillary muscle.

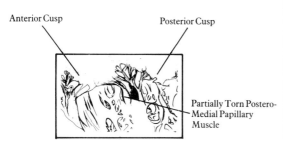

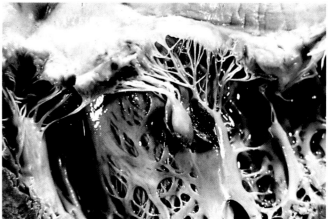

10   The left ventricle has been opened to show a papillary muscle infarct resulting in mitral regurgitation. The posterior papillary muscle is pale and shrunken due to infarction. The anterior papillary muscle (normal) is larger and darker. Subendocardial ischaemic scarring is present in the left ventricle.

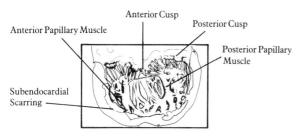

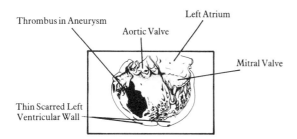

11   Widespread ischaemic scarring of the myocardium producing a dilated thin-walled ventricle. A thrombus has formed in one area in relation to the aneurysmal bulge of the ventricular wall.

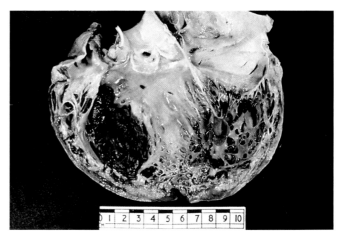

12   Localized left ventricular aneurysm due to ischaemic damage. The aneurysm does not contain more than a fine deposit of thrombus and has a larger central cavity opening into the ventricle.

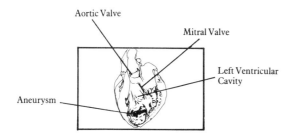

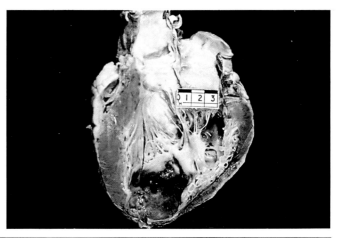

13 Chest radiograph showing an abnormal bulge on the left heart border due to a ventricular aneurysm. There is pulmonary oedema.

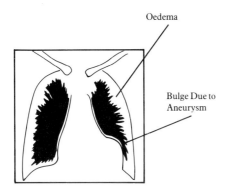

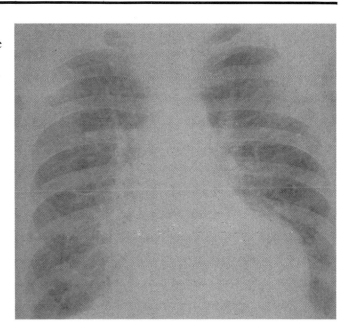

14 Chest radiograph showing pulmonary oedema and bilateral pleural effusions following acute myocardial infarction.

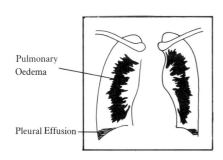

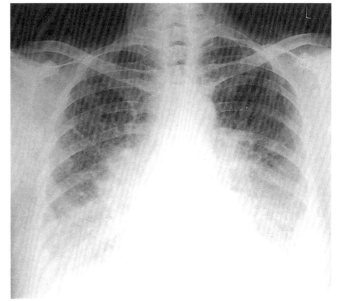

15 Chest radiograph showing cardiac enlargement with hilar oedema and generalized increase in pulmonary vessel size due to left-to-right shunt through a ventricular septal defect complicating myocardial infarction.

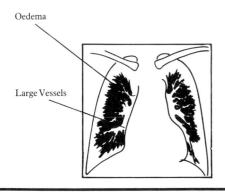

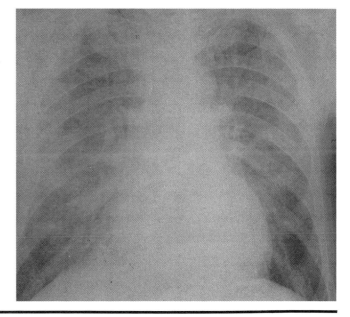

16 Chest radiograph of the same patient as [15] showing normal pulmonary vascularity following surgical closure of the defect.

Normal Vessel Size

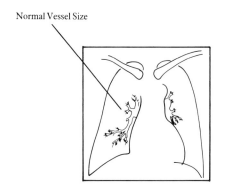

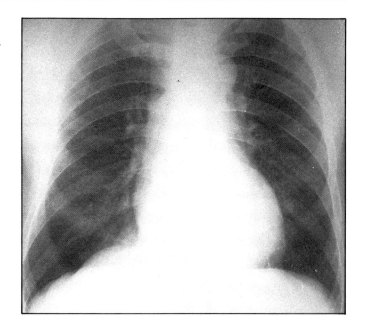

17

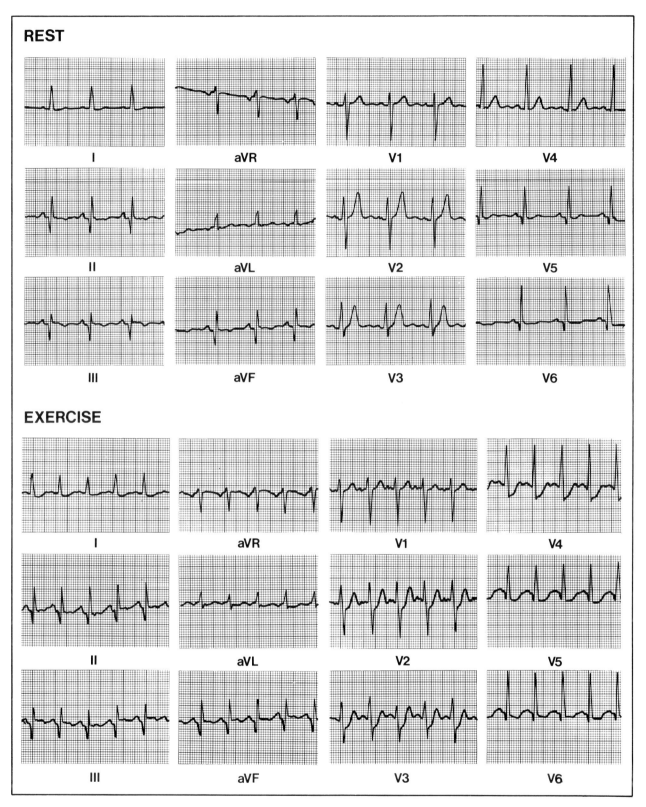

Resting and exercise electrocardiograms in a patient with angina. The resting electrocardiogram shows an old infero-lateral myocardial infarction. On exercise there is both horizontal and downsloping ST-segment depression in the anterior chest leads associated with the development of chest pain.

18

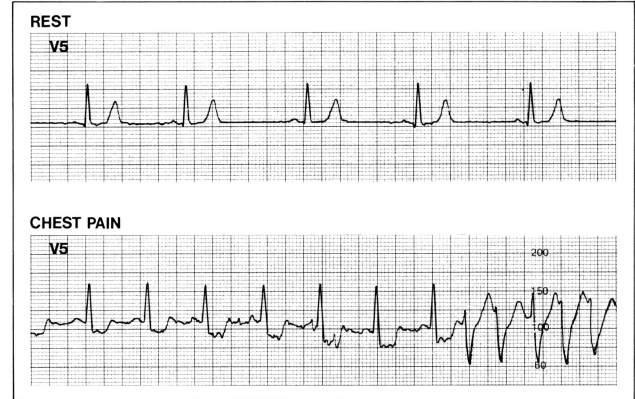

Electrocardiogram recorded during 24-hour ambulatory monitoring showing ST depression and the development of ventricular tachycardia during chest pain.

19

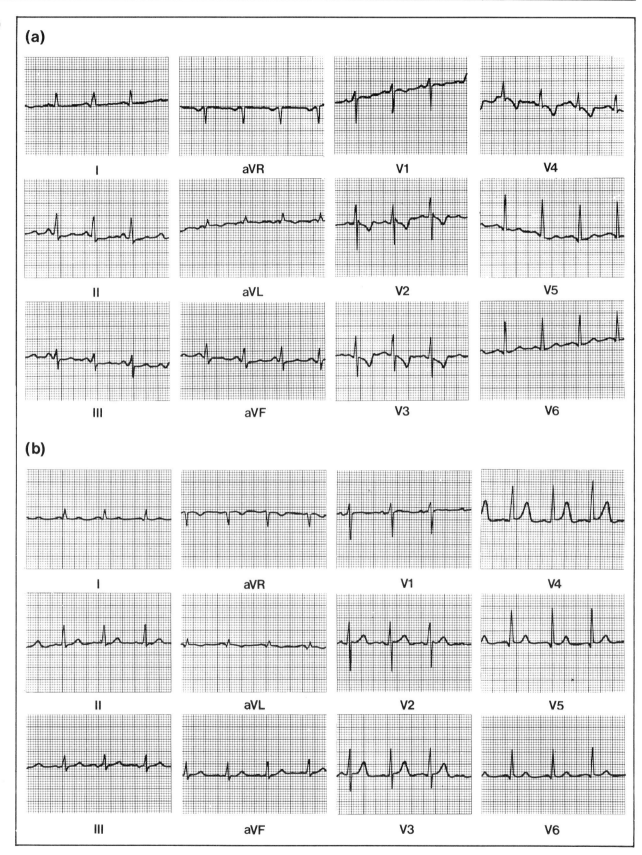

Resting electrocardiograms taken during chest pain in a patient with ischaemic heart disease showing ST-T wave abnormalities in the anterior chest leads (a). After the pain has subsided the ST-segment changes return to normal (b).

20

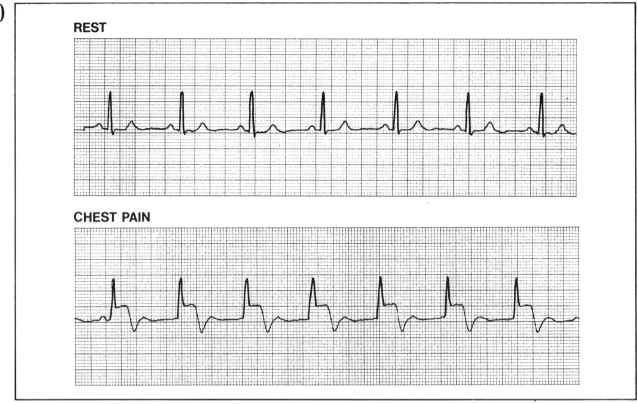

Electrocardiogram recorded during ambulatory monitoring showing ST-segment elevation during chest pain. During the episodes of myocardial ischaemia atrioventricular dissociation develops.

21

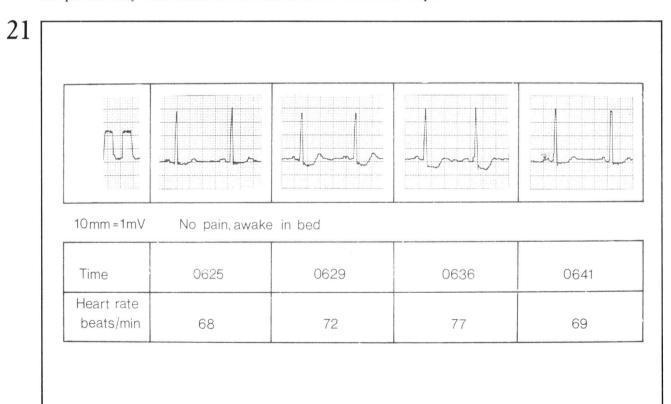

Electrocardiogram recorded during 24-hour monitoring. There are transient ST-segment changes whilst the patient was lying awake in bed. He did not complain of chest pain.

22

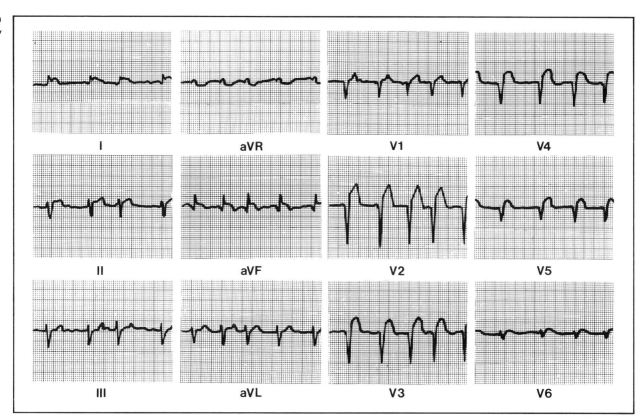

Electrocardiogram in a patient with acute antero-lateral myocardial infarction showing Q waves and ST elevation in V1–V4, I and aVL.

23

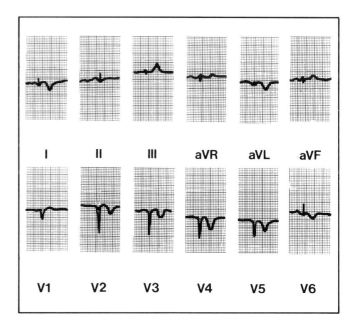

Electrocardiogram in the same patient as [22] taken several days later, showing T wave inversion in leads previously showing ST elevation with persisting Q waves.

24

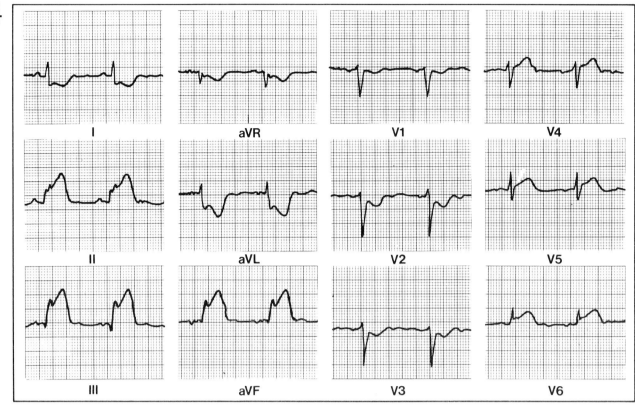

Electrocardiogram showing acute inferior myocardial infarction with ST elevation in II, III and aVF.

25

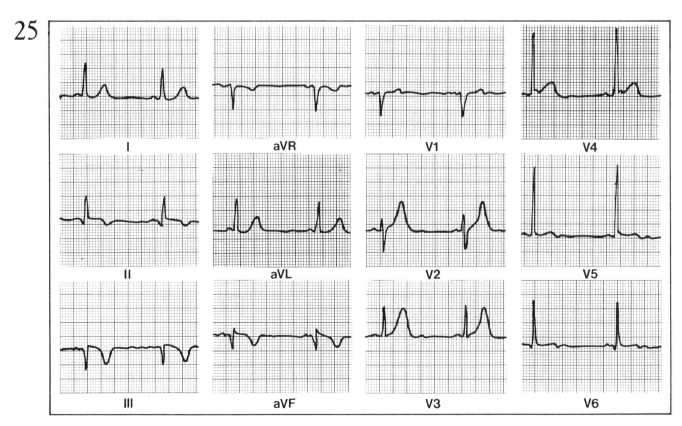

Electrocardiogram from the same patient as [24] showing Q waves and T wave inversion in leads II, III and aVF.

26

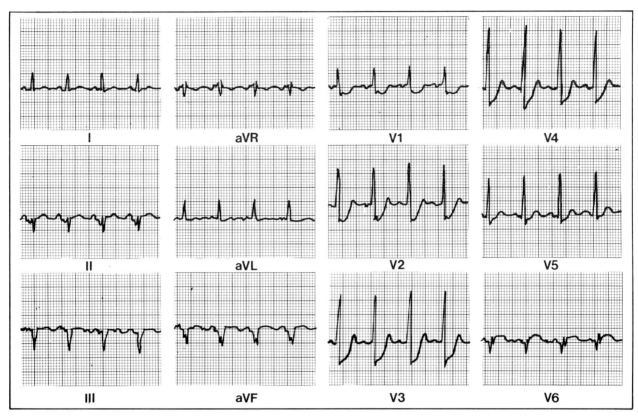

Electrocardiogram showing a true posterior myocardial infarction. There are Q waves in II, aVF and V6 with dominant R waves in V1-V4 together with ST-segment depression in the anterior chest leads.

27

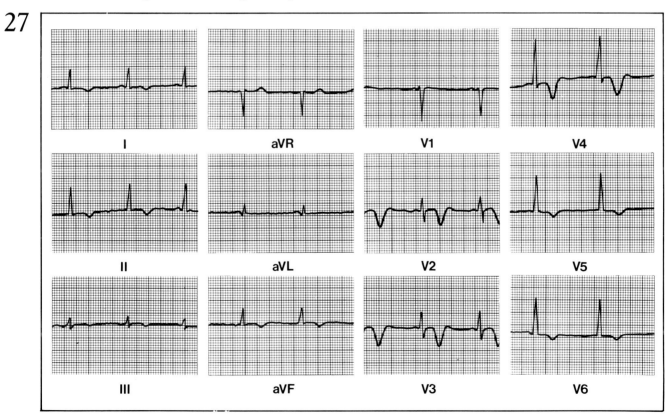

Electrocardiogram from a patient with a subendocardial infarction showing widespread T wave inversion.

28

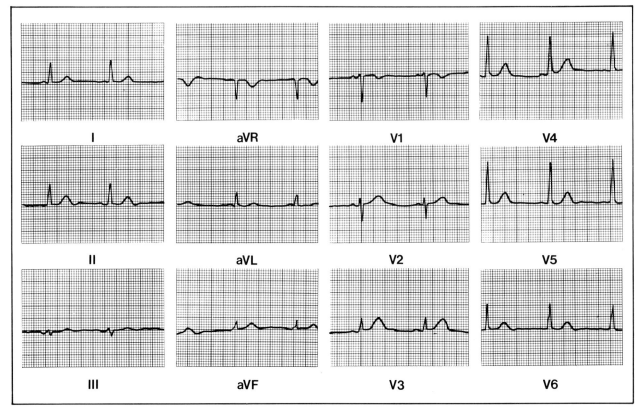

Electrocardiogram from the same patient as [27] several months later showing resolution of the T wave changes.

29

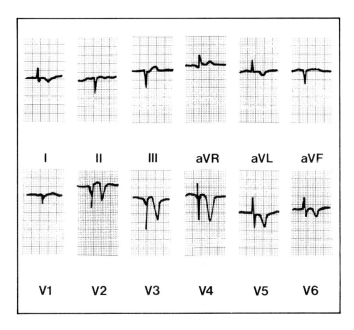

Electrocardiogram from a patient with a ruptured ventricular septum following myocardial infarction. There are Q waves in leads V1–V3 indicating septal infarction.

30

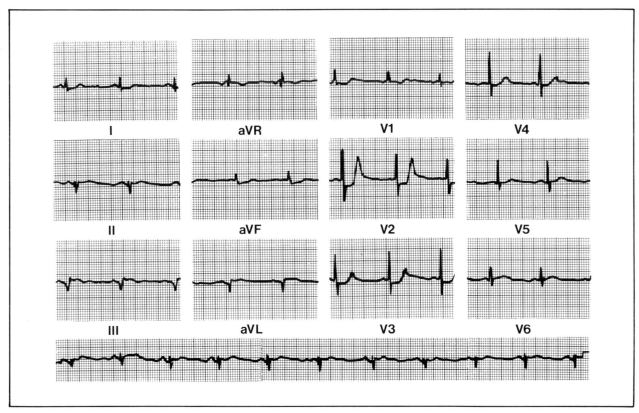

Electrocardiogram from a patient with mitral regurgitation secondary to inferior myocardial infarction. There are Q waves in the inferior leads, and incomplete right bundle branch block. The changes of true posterior infarction are also present.

31

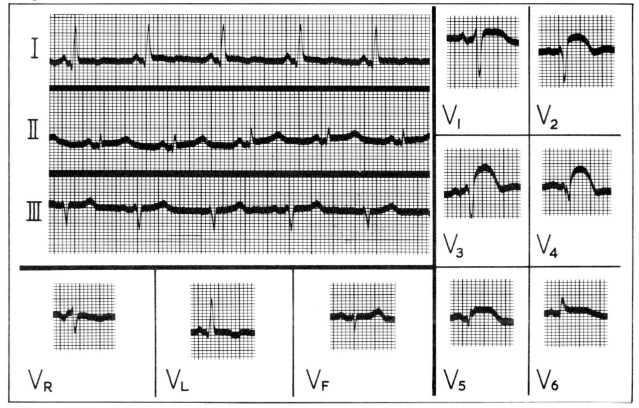

Electrocardiogram from a patient with a left ventricular aneurysm. There are Q waves and ST-segment elevation in the anterior leads some months following acute infarction.

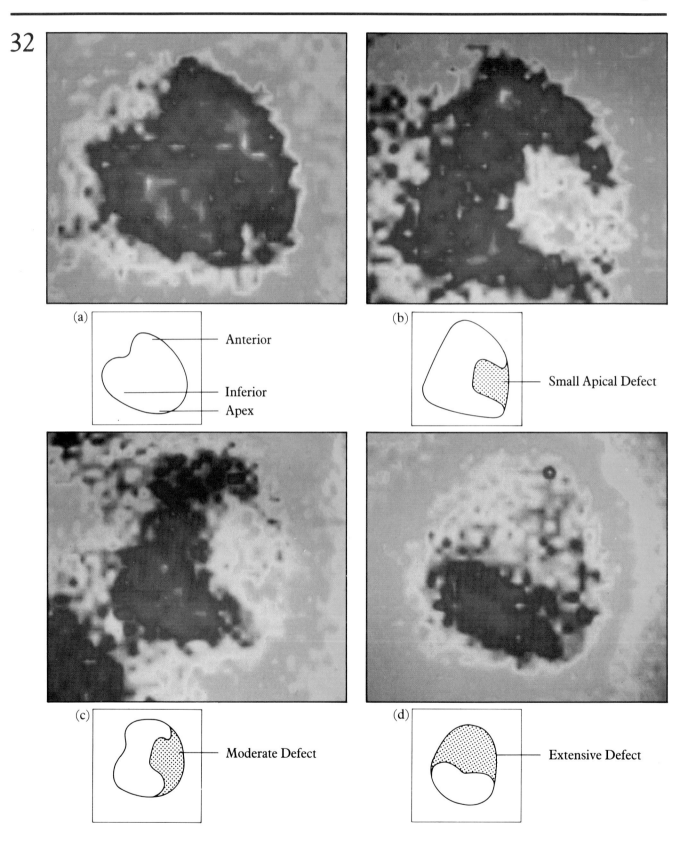

Thallium-201 scintigraphy, antero-posterior projection, recorded immediately after exercise; a) Normal appearance, b) Small apical defect, c) Moderate anterior and apical defects, d) Extensive defect affecting the whole of the anterior wall and apex.

33

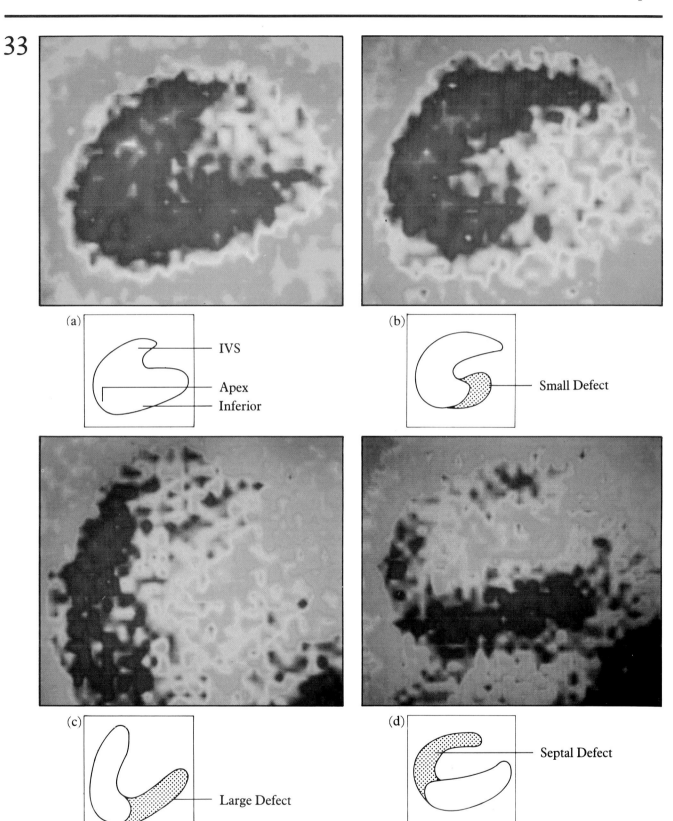

Thallium-201 scintigraphy, lateral projection, recorded immediately after exercise; a) Normal appearance, b) Small inferoposterior defect, c) Large inferior defect, d) Septal defect.

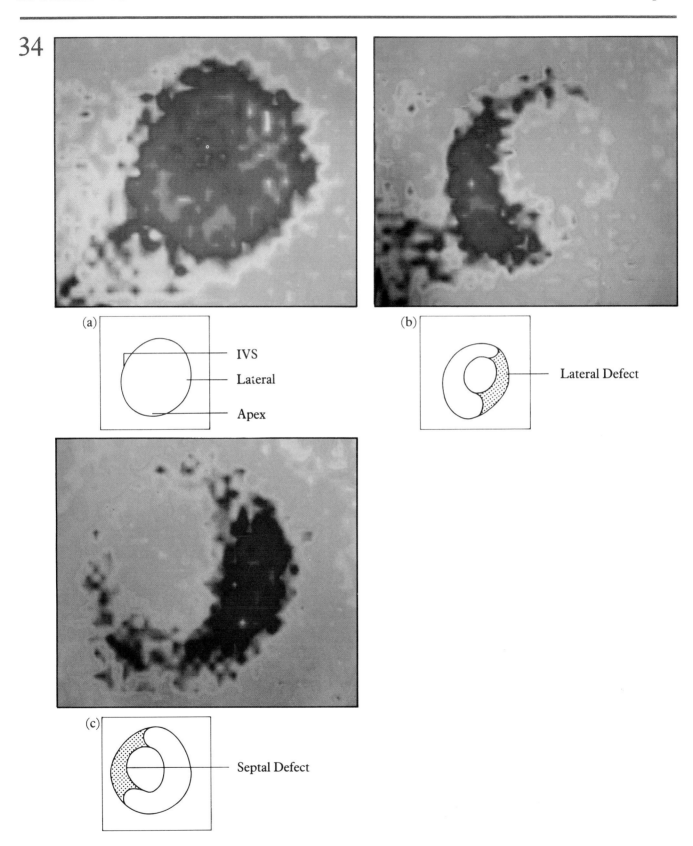

Thallium-201 scintigraphy, left anterior oblique projection, recorded immediately after exercise; a) Normal appearance, b) Lateral defect. The left ventricular cavity is dilated, c) and there is a septal defect.

35 Thallium-201 scintigraphy, left anterior oblique projection. Upper panel shows resting scintigram which is essentially normal apart from a small lateral defect. Lower panel shows scintigram recorded immediately after exercise in the same patient with a large lateral defect.

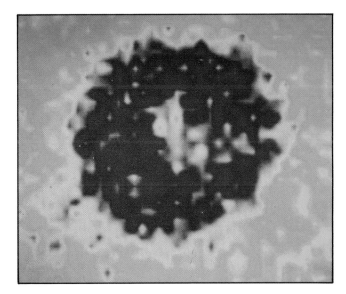

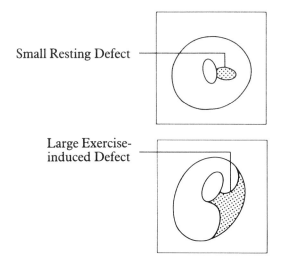

Small Resting Defect

Large Exercise-induced Defect

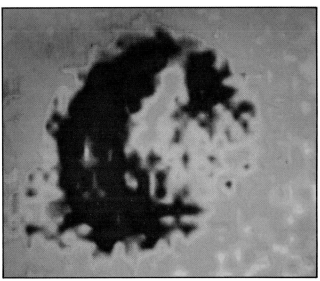

36

Normal uptake of technetium-99m labelled phosphate into the ribs and sternum. There is no myocardial uptake visible in any of the three standard views (antero-posterior, left anterior oblique and lateral).

37

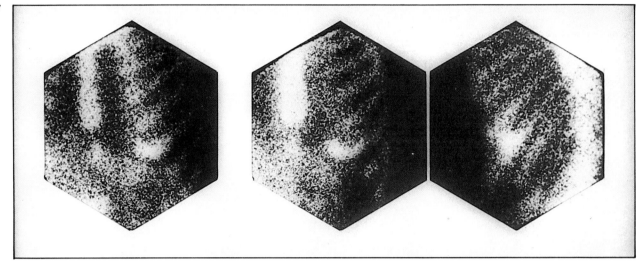

Uptake of technetium-99m labelled phosphate into acutely infarcted myocardium. This particular uptake pattern, which is suggestive of inferior wall myocardial infarction, can be seen in all three standard views.

38

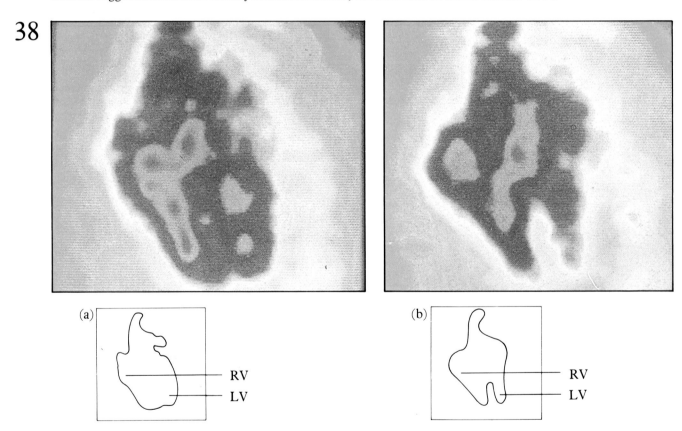

Gated blood pool image using technetium-99m labelled red cells in the left anterior oblique projection. End-diastolic (a) and end-systolic(b) frames are shown in a normal subject.

39 First pass study using technetium-99m in the left anterior oblique projection. End-diastolic (above) and end-systolic (below) images are shown in a normal subject.

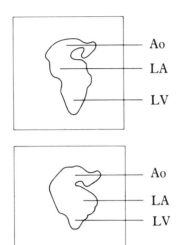

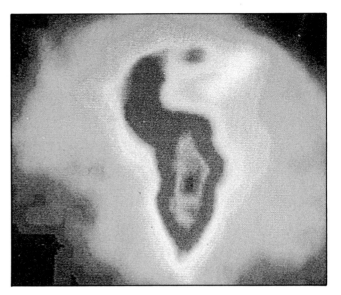

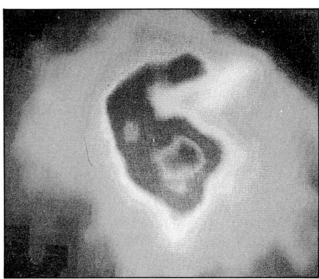

40 Gated blood pool image left anterior oblique projection in diastole in a normal subject (a), and in a patient with a left ventricular aneurysm (b).

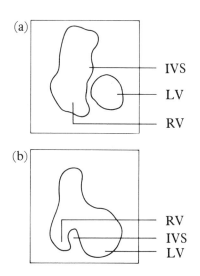

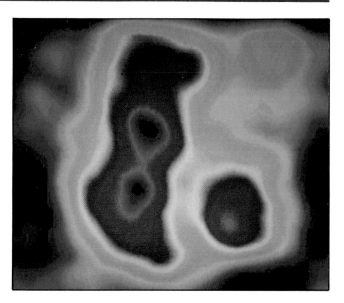

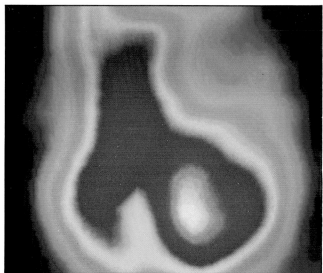

41

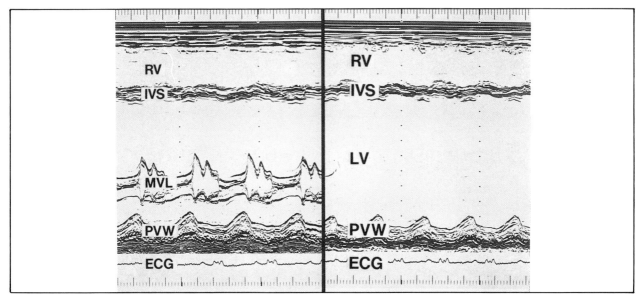

M-mode echocardiogram of the mitral valve (left) and left ventricle (right) in a patient with severe generalized left ventricular dysfunction due to coronary artery disease.

42

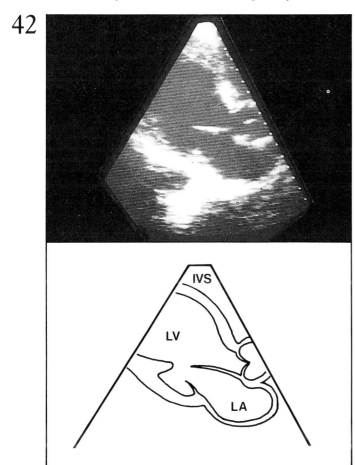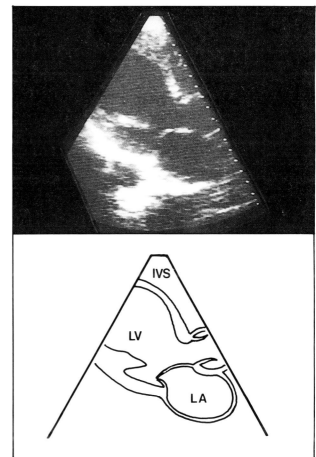

2-D echocardiographic parasternal long axis views in diastole (left) and systole (right) showing the thinning, anterior bulging and lack of movement of the septum following myocardial infarction.

43

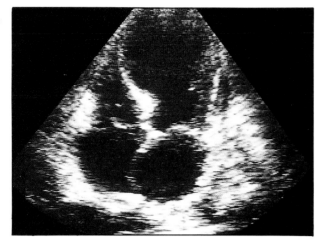 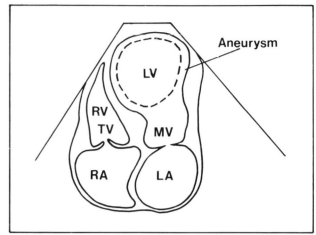

2-D echocardiographic apical four-chamber view of a large aneurysm.

44

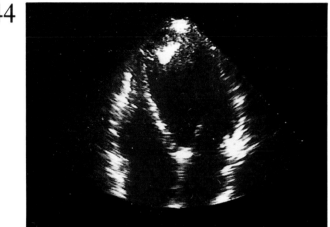 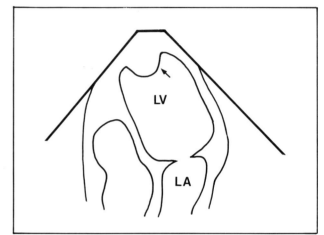

2-D echocardiographic apical four-chamber view of thrombus (arrow) in a patient with an old apical myocardial infarction.

45

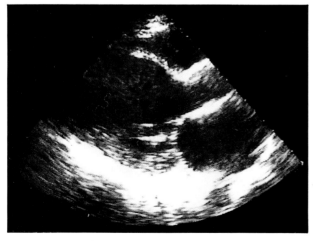 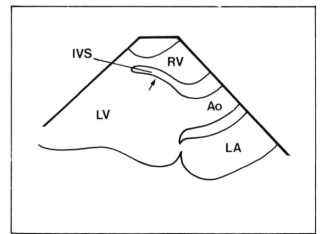

2-D echocardiographic systolic long axis view showing thinning of the septum (arrow) bulging into the right ventricle.

46

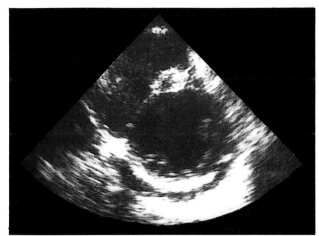 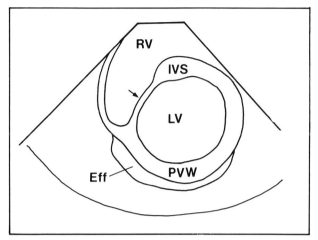

2-D echocardiographic systolic short axis view at level of papillary muscles in a patient with septal infarction. There is thinning of the septum (arrow) in relation to the anterior wall, and there is a pericardial effusion.

47

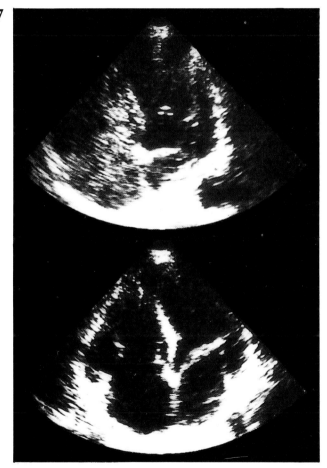 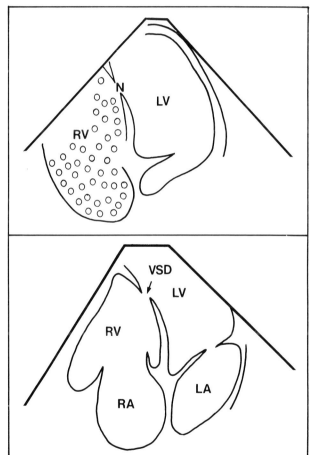

2-D echocardiographic four-chamber view in a patient with apico-septal ventricular septal defect after myocardial infarction. Above is a contrast injection into the right atrium and passing into the right ventricle ; there are some bubbles seen in the left ventricle . A negative contrast effect is seen in the right ventricle (N). Below is a non-contrast study in the same patient showing the ventricular septal defect (arrow) and a large right ventricle.

48

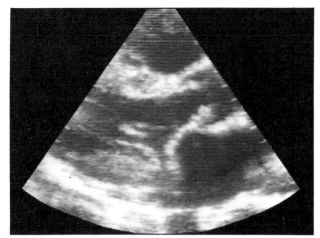
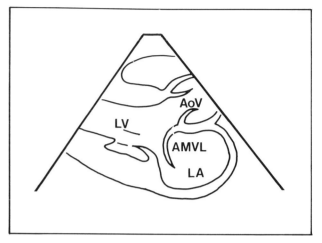

2-D echocardiographic parasternal long axis view showing 'flail' systolic motion of the anterior mitral valve leaflet into the left atrium.

ISCHAEMIC HEART DISEASE   Cardiac Catheterization & Angiography

49 Normal coronary arteriogram in the right anterior oblique view.

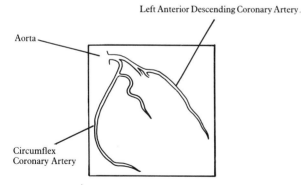
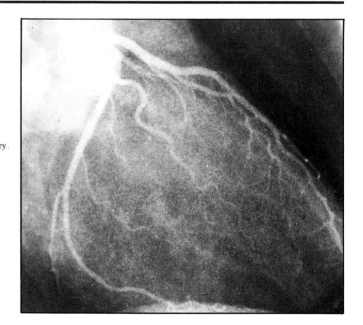

50 Angiogram in the left anterior oblique projection showing a normal left coronary artery.

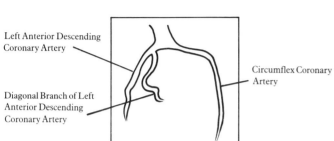

Left Anterior Descending Coronary Artery

Diagonal Branch of Left Anterior Descending Coronary Artery

Circumflex Coronary Artery

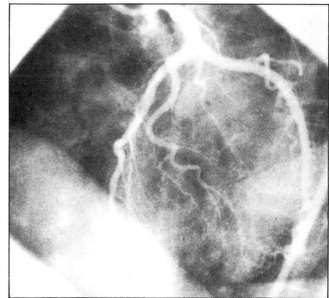

51 Angiogram in the right anterior oblique projection showing a normal right coronary artery.

Right Coronary Artery

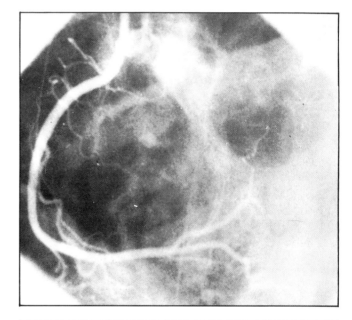

52 Angiogram showing atherosclerotic narrowing of the left anterior descending coronary artery (arrow).

Left Anterior Descending Coronary Artery

Circumflex Coronary Artery

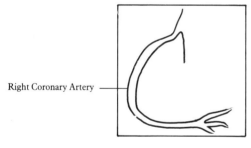

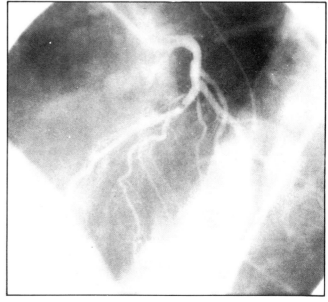

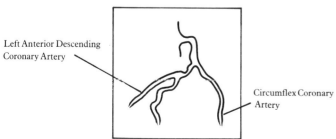

53 Angiogram showing atherosclerotic narrowing (arrow) of the left anterior descending coronary artery.

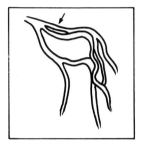

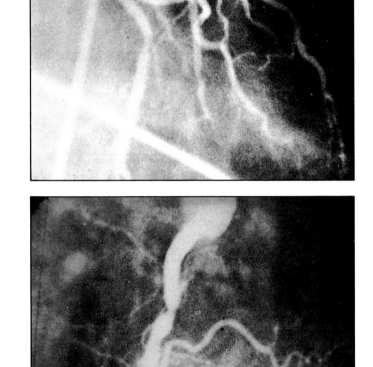

54 Right coronary angiogram viewed in the right anterior oblique projection showing obvious narrowing.

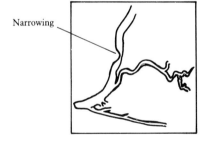

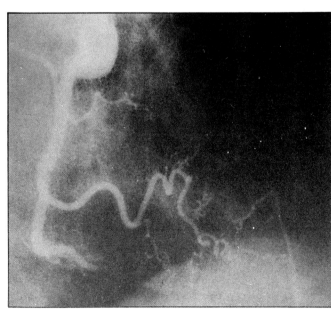

55 Right coronary angiogram viewed in the left anterior oblique projection showing diffuse disease of the artery with retrograde filling of the anterior descending coronary artery via septal collateral vessels.

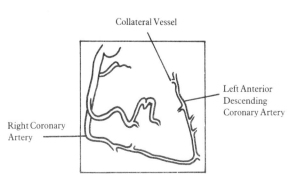

56

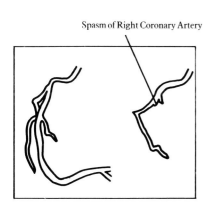

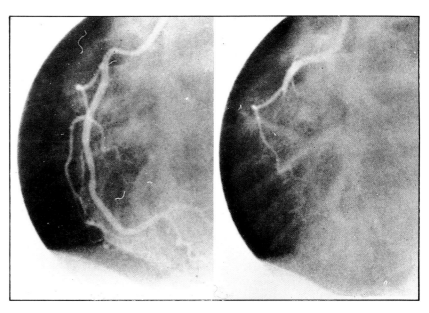

Coronary artery spasm. The angiogram on the left (left anterior oblique projection) shows normal blood flow in the right coronary artery. The angiogram on the right shows coronary artery spasm (arrow) completely occluding the right coronary artery.

57

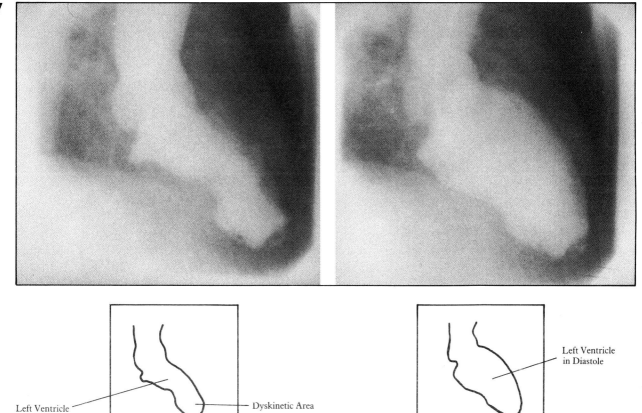

Left ventricular angiogram in the right anterior oblique projection. Systolic (left) and diastolic (right) frames reveal presence of apical dyskinesis and thrombus.

58

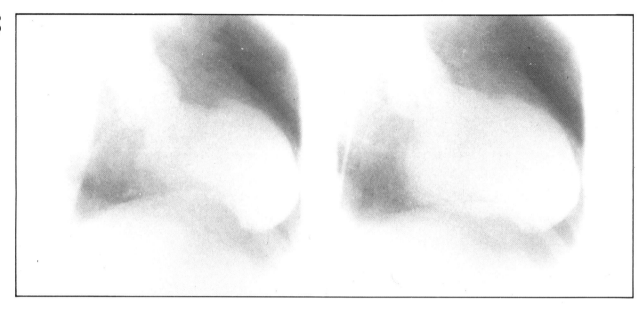

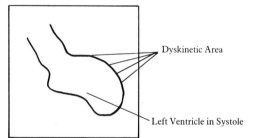

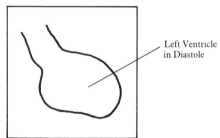

Left ventricular angiogram in the right anterior oblique projection with systolic (left) and diastolic (right) frames. It shows a large apical aneurysm with normal contraction of the remainder of the ventricle.

59

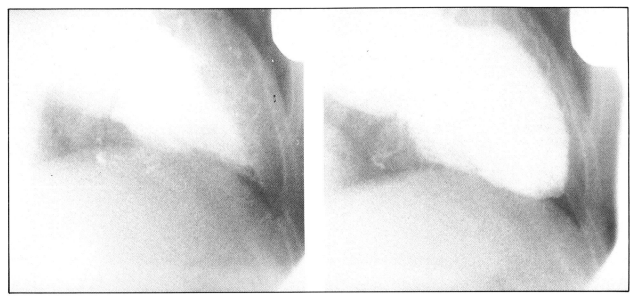

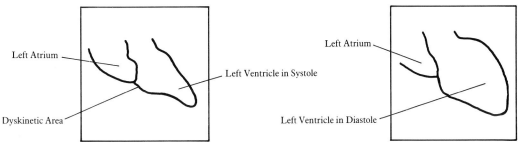

Left ventricular angiogram in the right anterior oblique projection with systolic (left) and diastolic (right) frames. It shows reduced contraction of the inferior wall of the left ventricle and dense opacification of the left atrium due to mitral regurgitation.

60 Left ventricular angiogram in the left anterior oblique projection showing a shunt from the left ventricle into the right ventricle due to rupture of the muscular septum.

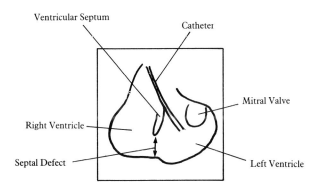

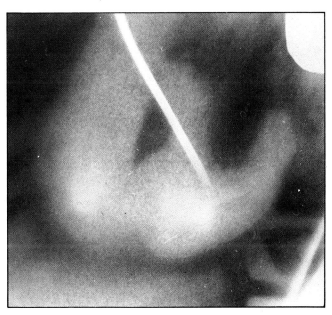